Seber
70

D1195184

G-13

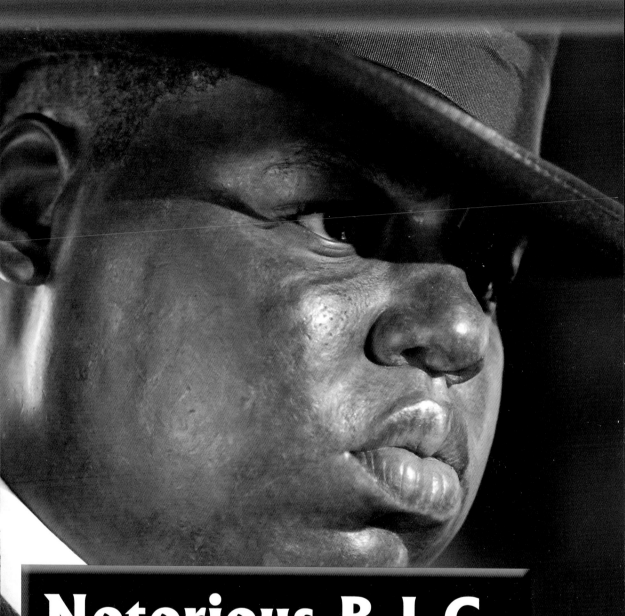

Notorious B.I.G.

by Z.B. Hill

Superstars of Hip-Hop

Alicia Keys

Beyoncé

Black Eyed Peas

Ciara

Dr. Dre

Drake

Eminem

50 Cent

Flo Rida

Hip Hop:
A Short History

Jay-Z

Kanye West

Lil Wayne

LL Cool J

Ludacris

Mary J. Blige

Notorious B.I.G.

Rihanna

Sean "Diddy" Combs

Snoop Dogg

T.I.

T-Pain

Timbaland

Tupac

Usher

Notorious B.I.G.

by Z.B. Hill

Mason Crest

Notorious B.I.G.

Mason Crest
370 Reed Road
Broomall, Pennsylvania 19008
www.masoncrest.com

Printed and bound in

First printing
9 8 7 6 5 4 3 2 1

Library of Congress Cataloging-in-Publication Data

Hill, Z. B.
  Notorious B.I.G. / by Z.B. Hill.
     p. cm. – (Superstars of hip-hop)
  Includes index.
  ISBN 978-1-4222-2524-0 (hard cover) – ISBN 978-1-4222-2508-0 (series hardcover) – ISBN 978-1-4222-9226-6 (ebook)
  1. Notorious B.I.G. (Musician)–Juvenile literature. 2. Rap musicians–United States–Biography–Juvenile literature. I. Title.
  ML420.N76H55 2012
  782.421649092–dc23
  [B]
                              2011020114

Produced by Harding House Publishing Services, Inc.
www.hardinghousepages.com
Interior Design by MK Bassett-Harvey.
Cover design by Torque Advertising & Design.

Publisher's notes:
• All quotations in this book come from original sources and contain the spelling and grammatical inconsistencies of the original text.
• The Web sites mentioned in this book were active at the time of publication. The publisher is not responsible for Web sites that have changed their addresses or discontinued operation since the date of publication. The publisher will review and update the Web site addresses each time the book is reprinted.

DISCLAIMER: The following story has been thoroughly researched, and to the best of our knowledge, represents a true story. While every possible effort has been made to ensure accuracy, the publisher will not assume liability for damages caused by inaccuracies in the data, and makes no warranty on the accuracy of the information contained herein. This story has not been authorized nor endorsed by Notorious B.I.G.'s estate.

Contents

Hip-Hop lingo

A **lyricist** is someone who writes the words in a song. The words are called "lyrics."

A **record** is a group of songs played on a plastic disc by a phonograph. Today, a lot of people still call CDs and MP3s "records."

A **feud** is a fight between two people or groups that goes on for a long time.

A **producer** is the person in charge of putting together songs. A producer makes the big decisions about the music.

A **label** is a company that produces music and sells CDs.

The **media** is the group of people who create news. Media can be photographs, videos, or news articles.

Rap is a kind of music where rhymes are chanted, often with music in the background. **Raps** are rhymes people make, sometimes off the top of their heads.

Chapter 1

Trouble at the Top

August 3, 1995, was a big night for Biggie Smalls, also known as Notorious B.I.G. He'd been invited to the Second Annual Hip-Hop Awards show—a pretty big deal for a 23-year-old hip-hop artist. The young man didn't look nervous, though. As usual, he was cool and laid back.

The awards rolled right in. Biggie won New Artist of the Year, **lyricist** of the Year, and Live Performer of the Year. He also earned one of the biggest honors of the night: Album of the Year.

In 1994, Biggie's album *Ready to Die* landed on the hip-hop scene like a bomb. With just one **record**, he changed hip-hop forever. The awards show was one way to recognize his hard work. It should have been one of the best nights of Biggie's life. But an ongoing **feud** between East and West Coasts made it not as good as it could have been.

East Coast Against West Coast

The feud began between Biggie's **producer** Puff Daddy and West Coast producer Suge Knight. By the time of the awards show, Suge and Puffy had been insulting each other for months. Things only got worse when both men were given a microphone at the awards show. When Suge took the stage, he insulted Puffy's habit of dancing in his stars' music videos. When Puffy took the stage, he tried to make peace. He said, "I'm a positive black man, and I want to bring us together, not separate us. All this East and West, that needs to stop. One love!"

But the fighting didn't stop. And Biggie got pulled into the mess. By 1994, there were two major hip-hop stars on the scene. One was signed to Suge Knight's **label**, Death Row Records. His name was Tupac Shakur. The other was Biggie, who was signed to Puffy's label, Bad Boy Entertainment. At first, both sides were friends. Suge and Puffy often shared business advice with each other. Tupac and Biggie were friends, too. One time, Tupac even invited Biggie on stage to rap with him. This was before Biggie was famous. Tupac spotted him in the crowd and called him up to the microphone.

But Suge Knight was not happy with the success of Bad Boy. *Ready to Die* had turned the attention away from the West and toward the East. In some people's minds, Puffy and Biggie had stolen Suge and Tupac's crowns. Suge accused Bad Boy of stealing Death Row's unique sound. On the night of the awards show, when Suge insulted Puffy in front of a huge crowd, he'd gone too far. After the show, the two groups met outside. There was an argument, and someone took out a gun. No one was hurt, but the damage was done.

Talk It Out?

The **media** started calling the fighting between the two labels the "East Coast–West Coast Rap War." It started as just a few insults. But it turned into something much bigger. The famous music pro-

Rappers Tupac Shakur (left) and Snoop Dogg (center) pose for a promotional picture with Suge Knight, head of Death Row Records. Knight's reputation as a dangerous man who surrounded himself with thugs and convicts gave the label credibility among fans of gangsta rap.

Puffy Combs and Notorious B.I.G. perform together during a concert. Though Combs was a talented and successful rap producer, Knight and others at Death Row made fun of Puffy's habit of joining his artists on stage or appearing in their music videos.

ducer Quincy Jones decided to step in and help. He called a meeting between the two sides.

Jones wanted to remind everyone that music should make the world a better place. He said that music should be used for peace, not violence. Many African-American leaders came to the meeting. Each speaker talked about power as a form of responsibility. This meant that people with power, like hip-hop artists, should use it to do good. But anger and violence continued to build. When the rappers left the meeting, nothing was settled.

Biggie told reporters he was not afraid of being attacked. "I'll be the cool dude," he said. "I have security, and they can handle that. I'm just the cool dude. Write the **raps**, do the shows, all that."

But as it turned out, Biggie had a lot to worry about.

Hip-Hop lingo

Poverty is when people are poor and cannot take proper care of themselves.

Mentors are people who teach someone else life lessons. They're usually older than the person they're helping.

DJ is short for disc jockey. A DJ plays music on the radio or at a party and announces the songs.

A **turntable** is the part of a phonograph (record player) that holds the plastic record and turns around under the needle. Sometimes a record player is called a turntable, too.

A **demo** is a rough, early version of a CD before the real thing comes out.

When a musician signs a **contract** with a music company, the musician promises to give all his music to that company for them to produce as CDs and then sell—and the music company promises to pay the musician a certain amount of money. Usually, a contract is for a certain period of time.

Chapter 2

Big Chris

Biggie's real name is Christopher Wallace. He was born May 21, 1972, in the Clinton Hill neighborhood of Brooklyn. Clinton Hill is a mix of a lot of different people. It has people of many skin colors and backgrounds. Most people who live there are very poor. Chris planned to rise above his **poverty** by becoming a rapper.

Chris's mother is Voletta Wallace. She moved to the United States from Jamaica, to be with Chris's father, George Latore. But soon after Chris was born, Voletta and George divorced. Voletta took night classes and got a job as a teacher. She provided Chris with a good home. She taught him to be a good student and made him work hard. By the time he was 11, Chris already had a job at a food market. He was a bright, happy, and talented young man. He did well in school, especially in art class. He hoped to go to college someday to study art. But then Chris discovered rap music, and all his plans changed.

Growing Pains

In the 1980s, rap was starting to gain strength. Many of the kids in Chris's neighborhood wanted to be rappers. Chris was no different.

He dreamed of hearing his voice on the radio. And he was talented, too. With some hard work, he might make it big in the rap game. Chris quickly made a name for himself by rapping for his friends and other neighborhood kids.

And it wasn't just his rap skills that made Chris hard to ignore. By the time he was a teen, he stood six feet two inches tall and weighed more than 300 pounds. People called him "Big Chris."

Pretty soon, Chris found himself in trouble with the law. Usually his crimes were small. He'd be brought to the police station, asked a few questions, and then let go. One police officer, Andre Parker, remembers talking to the young man. He told the story to Cathy Scott, author of *The Murder of Biggie Smalls*. "Yeah, he'd have a fit when we brought him in. He'd cry and say, 'I ain't doin' nothin'. I swear it.' He was just this chunky kid. A scared kid," said Parker. Sometimes Chris would tell the officers, "I'm gonna be famous one day. You wait 'n' see. I'm gonna be *big*."

"That Is Not Music!"

Voletta Wallace begged her son to stay out of trouble. But she found it harder and harder to get through to him. By the time he was 14, Chris's teachers said he was skipping classes. Up until his teen years, he'd been an amazing student. He worked hard and even helped other students with their schoolwork. But now that changed.

One day, police came to visit Voletta Wallace at home. They told her that Chris had been skipping school for weeks. Voletta was shocked. She sent Chris to school every day with his books. But he didn't go to school. He stashed his books on the roof and went wherever he wanted.

Voletta talked to Chris about his actions. "It turned uglier and uglier," Voletta wrote in her book. Biggie was slowly but surely choosing the streets. But he was also choosing music. This also confused Voletta. She didn't understand rap. When she heard her son's deep, husky voice, she thought it was a bad thing. She didn't realize that rappers have many different voices. She didn't know that her son's voice would someday be famous!

In her book, Voletta tells about days when Chris would play his music. "The noise was incredible. There was loud talking and then loud music, then loud talking and then banging on the furniture. I would say to myself, 'What is going on in my house?'" She even told Chris she didn't think he could sing. "That is *not* music! That's noise," she told him.

Christopher's mother, Voletta Wallace, worked as a teacher and hoped her son would get a good education. She did not like or understand rap music, which had just emerged as an art form during the late 1970s, when Chris was a little boy.

Slowly, Voletta began to see her son's talent. She still didn't understand hip-hop. But she saw the crowds of kids who gathered to hear Chris rap. She knew he was doing something special. She could accept her son's love for this strange new music. What really bothered her about Chris was not hip-hop. It was his choice not to stay in school.

Big Trouble for Big Chris

For a while, Chris did stay in school. In high school, he was even a Big Brother to younger kids with troubles. One of the men who worked at Chris's school was named Robert Izzo. In *The Murder of Biggie Smalls*, Izzo talks about Chris's skill as a **mentor**. "He worked well with kids, the younger ones. He didn't talk down to them."

But Chris continued to cut class. Finally, when he was in tenth grade, he dropped out. "I knew he was never going back to school," Voletta wrote. "We battled over this for three months. He cried and I cried. He cried and I cried some more. Then he stopped coming home."

Chris fell in with a bad crowd. He took on the role of a tough, street kid. He started selling drugs. He later told MTV about those days. "I was a full-time, one hundred-percent hustler. Sellin' drugs, wakin' up early in the morning . . . My mother goin' to work would see me out there in the morning. That's how it was."

Things got worse and worse for Chris. His mother was forced to watch him make his mistakes. Then he made a mistake he couldn't fix by himself. Chris visited some friends in North Carolina. He was arrested for selling drugs there. The police were not willing to let him out. So this time, Voletta had to pay $25,000 to bail him out. She used all the money she'd been saving for Chris's college education.

When he got out of jail, Chris promised his mother he was done selling drugs.

BIGGIE

VOLETTA WALLACE REMEMBERS HER SON, CHRISTOPHER WALLACE, AKA NOTORIOUS B.I.G.

Voletta Wallace

with Tre McKenzie

Foreword by Faith Evans

Voletta Wallace has published a book about her son. "Christopher was a man with a conscience," she wrote in *Biggie: Voletta Wallace Remembers Her Son* (2005). "He was a giver to anyone who asked. He was a man of his word. And he was always loyal."

Getting Serious About Hip-Hop

Chris kept his promise. He decided to put his energy into music, not drugs. He started spending time at his friend Chico Delvico's house. Chico loved hip-hop as much as Chris did. Chico wanted to be a **DJ**. He owned **turntables** and other stuff for making beats. Chris and Chico spent hours trying out rhymes and beats. They made **demos** of their music.

People often gathered to hear Christopher Wallace perform his rhymes over the beats of popular songs. He soon began to collaborate with a friend, Chico Delvico, who had created a small recording studio in his mother's home.

Chris began to attract a lot of attention. People in the neighborhood already liked his music. Now he had a demo to give them. They could play it at home or in their cars. Another Brooklyn rapper named Mister Cee decided to help Chris. He told Chris he'd give his demo to a hip-hop magazine, called *The Source*. The magazine loved the demo! They wrote a great article about Chris's music. They called him an exciting new voice in "gangsta rap."

Puffy Needs a Gangsta

Gangsta rap talked about life on the streets. It was just becoming popular in the late 1980s and early '90s. It was also starting to make some people very rich. A man named Puff Daddy was one of the producers who wanted to cash in on gangsta rap. When he heard Chris's demo, he knew this kid had talent. Puffy later told MTV about the first time he heard the demo. "As soon as I put it on, it just bugged me out. I listened to it for days and days, hours and hours."

Puffy hurried to meet Chris and offer him a record **contract**. When he met Chris, he was surprised by his size. Puffy was a businessman. He wasn't sure how to sell Chris's image to the world. But he knew he'd find a way.

He told Chris he would need a rap name. He wanted him to try something gangsta. One of Chris's favorite movies had a gangster named Biggie Smalls. The name made Chris laugh, so he decided to use it. And just like that, history was born.

Hip-Hop lingo

Something that is **classic** is likely to be popular for a long time.
A **studio** is a place where musicians go to record their music and turn it into CDs.

Chapter 3

Ready to Die

Fame didn't come overnight. Puffy had a plan for Biggie. Puffy wanted the young rapper to take things slow. At first, he only let Biggie rap on other artists' songs. It wasn't easy, but Biggie agreed to wait.

Then, things took a turn for the worse. Puffy was fired from his label! It looked like Biggie's dream could be over before it even started. The one man connecting him to stardom had just been fired from his label. And how could Biggie be a star without a label?

But Biggie didn't give up on Puffy. And for good reason! The young Puffy had a lot of talent as a producer. He seemed to have a magic touch when it came to turning unknown rappers into stars. So Puffy started his own label, called Bad Boy Entertainment. And he decided to make Biggie his first project. They started work on Biggie's first album, *Ready to Die*.

Cheo Coker has written a book about Biggie, called *Notorious*. Coker talks about why Biggie called his first album "ready to die." Biggie said, "I'm just trying to say that I'm ready to die for this. . . .

This is urgent. You got to be willing to do whatever you got to do to make this paper [money]."

Ready to Die was a huge hit. Critics called it a hip-hop **classic**. It instantly turned Biggie into a star. The album went on to sell millions of copies. It brought Biggie fame as well as riches.

There was one drawback, though. Biggie couldn't put the name "Biggie Smalls" on his records. There was already another artist using that name. So Biggie and Puffy decided to use "Notorious B.I.G." instead.

Notorious B.I.G. holds an award for his first album, *Ready to Die*. The record, released in 1994, was an immediate success. It contained several hit singles, sold more than four million copies, and was praised by many critics.

Gangsta Rap

The lyrics on *Ready to Die* made a lot of people upset. They were true to the gangsta life. They talked about murder, robbery, and treating women badly. It was pretty harsh stuff. But Biggie said he was just writing about what he saw in the world. Cathy Scott writes about this in her book about Biggie. She remembers him saying, "If I'd a worked at McDonald's, I'd a made rhymes about Big Macs and fries and stuff like that. I'm in Brooklyn. I see hustlin', I see killin', I see gamblin', I see girls, I see cars. That's what I rap about."

But people had a hard time accepting gangsta rap. On the West Coast, gangsta rap had made a lot of people angry. One West Coast rapper named Ice-T made a song about hurting policemen. Many people thought this went too far. It gave gangsta rap a bad name.

Some people said that gangsta rap sent the wrong messages to kids. They said rap lyrics tell kids that it's okay to treat women badly or to hurt other people. But the anger against gangsta rap didn't hurt Biggie's record sales. If anything, it helped. People wanted to listen to the music that was causing such excitement.

Success Brings Problems

Being a star means performing at lots of concerts. Biggie took his music to cities around the country. It wasn't always easy. Biggie was still a new star. Bad Boy was still a new label. Bad Boy didn't always have enough money to tell people about Biggie's shows. So sometimes Biggie would rap for a crowd of only ten or thirteen people. This was a big letdown for someone who'd sold over 4 million albums. Biggie worried his days of fame might be over.

But they were just getting started. People kept buying his music. And he never knew what to expect. In some cities, he'd rap for a crowd of hundreds of people.

The only threat to Biggie's success was himself. He'd started to live the gangsta life he rapped about. A few times, he was arrested for drugs and violence. But Biggie promised himself this would stop. He knew he needed to change his life.

Despite his success, Biggie could not avoid problems with the law.

Back to Basics

Biggie went back to the Brooklyn streets where he grew up. He began taking long walks in his old neighborhood. He even stopped to talk to young people. He would give money to some of them, and he'd tell them to stay away from drugs.

He also became interested in family life. He already had a daughter, T'yanna Wallace. She was born in 1993 to Biggie's girlfriend Jan Jackson. Biggie and Jan split up shortly after T'yanna was born. Then, in 1995, Biggie met Faith Evans. She was a musician, like Biggie. The two fell in love. They got married just eight days after they met! A year later, Faith gave birth to a baby boy, named C.J.

Biggie and Faith didn't have a good marriage. Biggie said they had married too quickly. But Biggie wanted to be a good father. He wanted to see both his kids grow up happy. "I want to go to my daughter's wedding. I want to go to my son's wedding," he told *Vibe* magazine.

Meanwhile, he went back to the **studio**. He started work on his next album, called *Life After Death*. It would definitely still be gangsta. But it would also be about Biggie's new outlook. The songs "Sky Is the Limit" and "Miss U" were about Biggie's love for his kids.

Little did Biggie know, *Life After Death* would be his last album.

Chapter 4

The Rap War

People from both sides of the rap war had a lot in common. Suge Knight was the head of Death Row Records. Puff Daddy was the head of Bad Boy Entertainment. Both men had grown up poor. Both had worked hard to gain power in the music business. Death Row's star was Tupac. Bad Boy's star was Biggie.

The two rappers also had a lot in common. Tupac and Biggie both came from rough neighborhoods. They'd both struggled to survive. They both wrote about life on the streets. Their lyrics described scenes of violence and death.

No one expected a war to break out between the two sides. In fact, many people say that the so-called war was really little more than a few fights. So what really happened?

Growing Tensions

At first, the war was no more than a few insults. Part of gangsta rap is looking tough and acting tough. Hip-hop artists will put down other hip-hop artists in their songs. It's just a part of the music. Usually, it's

Sean Combs and Suge Knight ignored each other on a sidewalk in Beverly Hills. By mid-1996, it seemed likely that the war of words between Bad Boy Entertainment and Death Row Records would soon take a violent, tragic turn.

Biggie speaks at the 1996 *Soul Train* Music Awards in Los Angeles. According to newspaper reporters, Biggie and Tupac confronted each other while backstage at the show. However, the two rappers denied the incident occurred.

all in good fun and no one really wants to hurt anyone else. Tupac and Biggie were no different. They said some harsh words, but in the end, it was mostly a game.

Then all that changed. On September 24, 1995, Biggie and Puffy went to a party in Atlanta. Suge Knight also went to the party. Both crews brought their bodyguards. One of Suge's bodyguards got into a fight with one of Puffy's bodyguards. Angry words were shouted. Someone pulled a gun and shot Suge's bodyguard, a man named Jake Robles. One week later, Jake died. Suge blamed Puffy for the death. He claimed Puffy had ordered the shooting.

Suge Knight's Death Row Records became a major label with the success of Dr. Dre's 1992 album *The Chronic*, a hip-hop classic that helped launch the career of Snoop Dogg. However, Knight's heavy-handed methods often got him into trouble with the law.

One year earlier, Tupac had been shot five times in New York City. He didn't know who ordered the shooting. But he thought it might be Biggie. The East Coast rapper denied that it was his fault. He said he had nothing to do with the shooting. But Tupac never fully trusted Biggie after that day.

Suge Knight didn't trust Puffy. Tupac didn't trust Biggie. It was producer against producer, and rapper against rapper. Things were starting to fall apart. At a 1996 awards show, Biggie and Tupac met backstage. They said some angry words. The friendship that once existed was gone.

Tupac's Death

Six months after the awards show fight, Tupac and Suge were in Las Vegas. They watched a boxing match, then left to go to a party. On the way out of the boxing match, they saw a man who belonged to a gang called the Crips. The Crips had an enemy gang called the Bloods. Many people said that Suge Knight was a member of the Bloods. When Tupac and a few bodyguards saw the Crips member, they attacked him. Some people said that Suge joined the attack. Then they left the building, got into their cars, and headed for the party.

Suge and Tupac got into the same car, with Suge in the driver's seat. When they pulled to a stop at a red light, another car pulled up beside them. A window rolled down, a gun pointed out, and shots were fired. Suge wasn't hurt, but Tupac was hit many times. He died a few days later.

Even today, people still blame Biggie and Puffy for the murder. But no one knows for sure who attacked Tupac that night. It could have been a Crips gang member. A lot of people think the Crips are responsible for Tupac's death. Or it could be someone else. After all, Tupac made many enemies in his short life.

The way the "rap war" story is usually told, it sounds like the West Coast and the East Coast wanted to kill each other. But trading insults and pushing and shoving backstage are a long way from ordering someone's murder. No one has ever proven that anyone from the East Coast rap scene killed Tupac.

Tupac was gunned down in Las Vegas on September 7, 1996, and died six days later. Some people suspected Biggie was involved in the murder because of their feud. Biggie and his friends claimed he was at home in New Jersey when the shooting occurred.

All Eyes on Biggie

Meanwhile, Biggie tried to stay out of the mess. He was busy making *Life After Death*. When he was invited to the *Soul Train* Music Awards in Los Angeles, he accepted. People booed at him from the crowd when he took the stage. After Tupac's death, Biggie was not very popular on the West Coast.

After the show, Biggie went to a party. He stayed at the first party for a few hours before deciding to go to another party. He climbed into the passenger seat of a car. Two of Biggie's friends climbed into the backseat. Biggie put on a tape of *Life After Death*. He wanted to see if it needed any last-minute changes. Then the car pulled away from the hotel.

But they didn't get far. At the first red light, a black car pulled up next to them. A hand reached out of the window, holding a gun. Seven shots were fired. All seven hit Biggie. He slumped over in his seat. The gunman's car zoomed away.

Puffy was with Biggie that night. He was riding in a car just behind Biggie's. When he heard the shots, Puffy jumped out of his car and ran toward him. Puffy later told the *New York Daily News* about what happened next. "I was saying the Lord's Prayer and Hail Marys. I was begging God to help him out. I was touching him and talking to him in his ear."

But there was nothing Puffy could do. One hour later, Biggie was dead.

XXL

IN STEREO

THE MAKING OF
LIFE AFTER DEATH

Hip-Hop lingo

To **mourn** is to be sad because someone has died.
Critics are people who judge artistic works and say what is good and what is bad about them.
A **charity** is a group that gives time, money, or other things to help make people's lives better.

2-1997

NOTORIOUS B.I.G
THE LOST TAPES

Chapter 5

Life After Death

Biggie's funeral was held near his childhood home in Brooklyn. Cars lined up and people crowded into the streets. When the line of cars passed Biggie's old house, people noticed two little girls holding a sign. It read, "We love you, Biggie. Save our youth. Stop the violence."

Some of rap's biggest stars came to Biggie's funeral. DJ Kool Herc, Foxy Brown, Queen Latifah, and Mary J. Blige were there. There were also members of the Junior M.A.F.I.A. there that day. The Junior M.A.F.I.A. was a group of young rappers that Biggie helped become famous. He had produced their first album.

Puffy read a few words in memory of Biggie. Then Faith Evans sang the song "Walk With Me, Lord."

Reporters mixed with the crowd. They wanted to know why hundreds of people came to **mourn** the death of a rapper. A woman named Carol Williams told *People* magazine about what Biggie meant to people from Brooklyn. She said, "They're here to express love. It's like when John F. Kennedy passed on. Biggie may not have been presidential material, but to the extent that he was able to come from this way of life and succeed, he means a lot to people."

The Music Lives On

Just two weeks after Biggie died, *Life After Death* hit stores. It went straight to the top, selling 700,000 copies in the first week. Eventually, it sold more than 5 million copies. Not only did it sell well,

Biggie was mourned by tens of thousands of fans. Many gathered on the streets of New York to observe his funeral procession on March 18, 1997. This photo was taken in the Bedford-Stuyvesant neighborhood of Brooklyn.

A group of Biggie's friends and family members accept an award on his behalf at the MTV Video Music Awards ceremony in September 1997. Biggie's song "Hypnotize," one of several hit singles from *Life After Death*, was named Best Rap Video.

but **critics** liked it too. Some people said that it was even better than *Ready to Die*.

There was no doubt about it: Biggie had created another hit album. He was a hip-hop star, even after death! Some of the songs from *Life After Death* became hip-hop classics. They included "Hypnotize," "Going Back to Cali," and the huge hit "Mo Money Mo Problems."

It didn't stop there. Bad Boy put out two more records of Biggie's music after his death. The first came out it 1999, called *Born Again*. It included many tracks that Biggie had recorded before he died. Puffy asked other artists to add to Biggie's tracks. He invited Busta Rhymes, Snoop Dogg, Redman, and Eminem to help finish what Biggie started.

In 2005, Bad Boy released *Duets: The Final Chapter.* It was made in about the same way as *Born Again.* Puffy chose new beats for Biggie's old tracks, and invited new artists to join him.

Who's Guilty?

A lot of effort has gone into finding Tupac and Biggie's killers. Many people have been accused. Some people say it was Suge Knight who killed both men. Other people say that Biggie ordered Tupac's killing. Still others say that Los Angeles policemen killed both rappers!

The court battles went on and on. Tupac's case was dropped, but not Biggie's. Both Voletta Wallace and Faith Evans spent many years in court trying to find Biggie's killer. For a while, Voletta and Faith seemed to have a case against two L.A. police officers. But in April 2010, the case against the two officers was dropped. We may never know who killed Tupac or Biggie.

Chris's Dream Lives On

No one knows what Christopher Wallace would have done if he survived those seven bullets. But one thing is for certain: his memory lives on. Voletta Wallace has made sure his love for young people is remembered.

Since Chris died, Voletta has used money from his album sales to create the Christopher Wallace Memorial Foundation. The **charity** gives money to inner city schools and other urban youth

Biggie's widow, Faith Evans, leaves a Los Angeles courtroom in July 2005. Evans and Voletta Wallace filed a lawsuit against the Los Angeles Police Department, alleging that renegade members of the department had been involved in Biggie's murder.

This publicity photo of Notorious B.I.G. was taken to promote the rapper's second album, *Life After Death*. Biggie was proud of the way the album had turned out, but did not live to see it released.

programs. Chris had an amazing talent. The foundation tries to help kids find their own talents and skills.

As Voletta Wallace says in her book, "Christopher had big, big dreams. He had a plan. He had a grand vision." Chris lived long enough to see that dream begin to come true. Maybe his life will help others realize their own dreams.

In 2012, 15 years after Chris's death, Jay-Z performed at New York City's famous Carnegie Hall. At the show, Jay-Z played Biggie's song "Juicy." Jay stood on the balcony of the concert hall in a dark suit. He barely had to rap at all. The crowd knew every word.

Jay gave a shout when fans rapped the line "You never thought hip-hop would take it this far." Thanks to Notorious B.I.G., hip-hop is one of the most popular forms of music in the world. Chris helped to make the music he loved into something much bigger than himself.

Chris may be gone. But he lives on in the music he left behind and in the hearts of hip-hop fans everywhere.

1972   Christopher Wallace is born on May 21, in the Clinton Hill neighborhood of Brooklyn, New York.

1989   Wallace drops out of school and becomes a small-time drug dealer.

1992   Wallace sends a demo tape to *The Source* magazine, which features him as a dynamic new talent on the hip-hop scene; Sean "Puffy" Combs signs Wallace to a contract with Uptown Records.

1993   Combs leaves Uptown Records and forms Bad Boy Entertainment; he signs Wallace to a recording contract under the name Biggie Smalls.

1994   *Ready to Die* is released under Biggie's new name, Notorious B.I.G. In November, rival rapper Tupac Shakur is shot as he enters the lobby of a New York recording studio. Shakur accuses Biggie of planning the assault, touching off the East Coast –West Coast Rap War.

1995   Biggie and *Ready to Die* win four awards at *The Source* magazine's Second Annual Hip-Hop Awards. Biggie is arrested for assault in cases in New York City and Camden, New Jersey. Biggie meets and marries R&B singer Faith Evans. In September, Death Row Records founder Suge Knight blames Combs for planning the murder of his associate, Jake "The Violator" Robles.

1996   A police raid on Biggie's home in Teaneck, New Jersey, uncovers guns and ammunition; Biggie is also charged with smoking marijuana in a car on a Brooklyn street. On September 7, Shakur is murdered in Las Vegas, Nevada.

1997   Biggie Smalls is murdered on March 9 after leaving a party in Los Angeles; his album *Life After Death* is released two weeks later.

1999 The album *Born Again* is released.

2001 Voletta Wallace and Faith Evans file a lawsuit against the Los Angeles police, alleging that members of the department assisted Suge Knight in the murder of Biggie.

2002 The *Los Angeles Times* publishes a series of stories alleging that Biggie paid $1 million to Crips member Orlando Anderson to kill Tupac Shakur.

2005 *Duets: The Final Chapter* is released; in June, the Wallace-Evans lawsuit comes to trial, but it is dismissed when U.S. District Judge Florence-Marie Cooper rules that the Los Angeles police withheld evidence from Biggie's mother and widow.

2006 Judge Cooper fines the Los Angeles police $1 million for withholding evidence.

In Books

Baker, Soren. *The History of Rap and Hip Hop*. San Diego, Calif.: Lucent, 2006.

Comissiong, Solomon W. F. *How Jamal Discovered Hip-Hop Culture*. New York: Xlibris, 2008.

Cornish, Melanie. *The History of Hip Hop*. New York: Crabtree, 2009.

Czekaj, Jef. *Hip and Hop, Don't Stop!* New York: Hyperion, 2010.

Haskins, Jim. *One Nation Under a Groove: Rap Music and Its Roots*. New York: Jump at the Sun, 2000.

Hatch, Thomas. *A History of Hip-Hop: The Roots of Rap*. Portsmouth, N.H.: Red Bricklearning, 2005.

Websites

Biggie Smalls
www.biggiesmalls.net

Faith Evans, Biggie's Widow
www.faithevansonline.com

FBI: Crips and Bloods
foia.fbi.gov/foiaindex/cripsbloods.htm

More on Biggie
www.cathyscott.com/biggie.htm

MTV: Biggie Smalls
www.mtv.com/music/artist/notorious_big/artist.jhtml

Discography

Albums

1994	Ready to Die
1997	Life After Death
1999	Born Again
2005	Duets: The Final Chapter

Index

Index

About the Author

Z.B. Hill is a an author and publicist living in Binghamton, New York. He has a special interest in adolescent education and how music can be used in the classroom.

Picture Credits

1: Dreamstime, Rorem
8: AP Photo/Mark Lennihan
9: NMI/Death Row Records
10: Everrett Collection
12: Photofest
15: Zuma Press/Nancy Kaszerman
17: PRNewsFoto/NMI
18: Photofest
21: Bad Boy Entertainment/NMI
22: Miramax/Photofest
24: AP Photo/Adam Nadel
27: Everrett Collection
28: Splash News
29: Reuters/Fred Prouser
30: KRT/Giulio Marcocchi
32: AFP/Death Row Records
34: NMI/Michelle Feng
36: KRT
37: AP Photo/Adam Nadel
39: Reuters/Mario Anzuoni
43: UPI Photo/Jim Ruymen

To the best knowledge of the publisher, all other images are in the public domain. If any image has been inadvertently uncredited, please notify Harding House Publishing Services, Vestal, New York 13850, so that rectification can be made for future printings.